DOGS SET VIII

NEWFOUNDLANDS

Jill C. Wheeler
ABDO Publishing Company

visit us at
www.abdopublishing.com

Published by ABDO Publishing Company, 8000 West 78th Street, Edina, Minnesota 55439. Copyright © 2010 by Abdo Consulting Group, Inc. International copyrights reserved in all countries. No part of this book may be reproduced in any form without written permission from the publisher. The Checkerboard Library™ is a trademark and logo of ABDO Publishing Company.

Printed in the United States of America, North Mankato, Minnesota.
092009
012010

 PRINTED ON RECYCLED PAPER

Cover Photo: Alamy
Interior Photos: Alamy pp. 15, 21; Animals Animals p. 11; Corbis pp. 7, 9;
    Getty Images pp. 10, 13, 17, 19; Peter Arnold p. 5

Series Coordinator: Tamara L. Britton
Editors: Heidi M.D. Elston, Megan M. Gunderson
Art Direction: Neil Klinepier

Library of Congress Cataloging-in-Publication Data

Wheeler, Jill C., 1964-
 Newfoundlands / Jill C. Wheeler.
    p. cm. -- (Dogs)
 Includes index.
 ISBN 978-1-60453-783-3
 1. Newfoundland dog--Juvenile literature. I. Title.
 SF429.N4W47 2010
 636.73--dc22   2926
                                 2009033467

CONTENTS

THE DOG FAMILY

All dogs belong to the family **Canidae**. The dog family is very **diverse**. Its members can be found on nearly every continent. Dogs come in many shapes, sizes, and personalities. There are more than 400 different **breeds**.

Dogs were first used to hunt. Over time, humans began breeding them for other activities. These included rescuing, herding, hauling, and guarding. Dogs and humans came to develop a special relationship. Today, dogs are often referred to as man's best friend.

The Newfoundland breed has a very special bond with humans. Throughout history, farmers and fishermen depended on these working dogs. Newfoundlands are loyal companions that live to please people.

The Newfoundland (far right) is one of the only dog breeds to appear on a postage stamp.

NEWFOUNDLANDS

The Newfoundland dog is affectionately called "Newf" or "Newfy." Its exact origin is uncertain. However, historians agree the **breed** began in Newfoundland, Canada. Many believe fishermen brought the dog's ancestors to the area in the 1600s.

The **American Kennel Club** recognized the Newfoundland breed in 1886. Newfs are classified as working dogs. In their early days, these large dogs worked alongside fishermen. The dogs pulled fishnets and swam fishing lines to shore. In addition, they hauled wood and other heavy items.

Newfoundlands are known for being strong swimmers. They have rescued men, women, and children from the water. Today, many kennel clubs host Newfoundland rescue exhibitions to recognize this ability and courage.

A Newfoundland named Seaman traveled with the Lewis and Clark Expedition. And, a Newfoundland starred as the nanny in the original *Peter Pan* play.

WHAT THEY'RE LIKE

Newfoundlands are among the largest dog **breeds**. But they are also among the most gentle. Newfs are patient and calm.

One of the Newf's best qualities is its sweet temperament. This large breed is great with children and friendly with guests and other pets. Another favorable quality Newfs have is their intelligence. This makes them easy to train.

Newfs have a social personality. So, it is important to treat them like members of the family. They do not enjoy being left alone.

Newfs are devoted, trustworthy, and obedient. They can recognize dangerous situations and act on

their own. This makes them good water rescue dogs. Newfs are also dependable guardians and watchdogs. They will take action to protect their families from danger.

In ancient times, Newfs often served as nannies to children. Today, they assist humans in rescue situations.

COAT AND COLOR

A majestic coat adds to the Newfoundland's size, nobility, and presence. The coat is thick and moderately long. Standard colors are black, brown, gray with some white, and Landseer. The Landseer Newf has a white base coat with black markings.

A Landseer Newf

Newfs shed their thick coat most heavily in spring. They shed again in fall.

The Newf has a double coat. The outer coat is stiff and oily. The undercoat is soft and fleecy. These features make the coat water resistant. In fact, a Newfoundland can comfortably swim in cold water. Its skin will remain dry and warm.

Other striking physical features include a massive head with a broad **muzzle**. The Newf has dark brown eyes that are deep set and small. Its face has a look of kindness and intelligence.

SIZE

These gentle giants weigh more than 100 pounds (45 kg) when mature! Male Newfoundlands weigh between 130 and 150 pounds (60 and 70 kg). Females weigh 100 to 120 pounds (45 to 55 kg). On average, males stand 28 inches (71 cm) tall at the shoulders. Females are 26 inches (66 cm) tall.

With a large, powerful body, Newfs are built for water and hard work. Their muscular build gives them the strength to swim in rough ocean waters. It also helps them pull and haul.

Newfs have a few other advantages in the water. Their lungs can take in lots of air. This helps them swim long distances. In addition, Newfs have loose **flews**. This allows them to breathe even when carrying someone or something.

Newfs also have large, webbed paws. And unlike other water-loving dogs, Newfs do not dog-paddle. Instead, they swim with a breaststroke. In this way, they waste less energy.

Newfs are often called gentle giants.

CARE

Regular exercise is important for the health and well-being of Newfoundlands. Because Newfs love water, swimming is a favorite exercise. A brisk daily walk is another fun activity.

The Newf's thick coat and large size make it important to watch for **heatstroke**. On hot days, Newfs should stay indoors or in shaded areas. And, they should have lots of fresh water.

It is also important to take care of Newf coats. They need to be brushed at least once a week. Even more brushing is required when they are shedding in spring and fall.

Hip problems and heart disease are common among this **breed**. So, regular visits with a veterinarian are important. Newfs should also stay

Newfs are always up for a swim!

current with their **vaccines**. And, the veterinarian can **spay** or **neuter** Newfs. At home, owners should check their dogs weekly for problems.

FEEDING

A proper diet is another important part of good health care for Newfoundlands. As a general rule, Newfs should be fed a high-grade dog food. And, they need plenty of fresh water at all times.

It is best to discuss diet and meal plans with a veterinarian. How much and what to feed Newfs varies with each dog. Growing puppies will eat more during growth spurts than they will as adults! Puppies may eat three to four small meals per day. Adults usually eat two meals a day.

Owners should carefully monitor their Newf's diet. This large dog should be prevented from becoming overweight.

Many Newfs enjoy chewing on rawhide bones.

THINGS THEY NEED

More than anything, Newfs need good, caring families. As social animals, they require attention. They bond quickly with their owners and are very loyal.

Because of their size, Newfs should be trained and **socialized** at an early age. Obedience training teaches Newfs to adjust their strength. This helps them avoid injuring anyone.

Newfs also need space. A large, fenced-in yard is recommended. They need room inside, too. This is not a good **breed** for an apartment.

Owners will need to provide a leash, a collar, a license, and identification tags. Every Newf also needs sturdy food and water bowls, a soft bed, and toys.

18

Newfs drool, slobber, and shed. Owners need to expect and accept this. The best Newf owners are active, patient, and loving.

Newfs are willing learners and want to please.

PUPPIES

Newfoundland dogs are **pregnant** for 63 days. Newfs average six to ten puppies in a **litter**. It is recommended to buy a puppy through a reputable **breeder**.

Just as people have different personalities, the same is true with dogs. When choosing your pet, look for playful, curious puppies. They should be willing to approach people and be held.

Diet is very important to Newf puppies. Proper feeding will help build strong bones and prevent joint problems. Newf puppies may also need a special diet to manage their growth rate.

Newfs can be great pets. Families must be accepting of their shedding, drooling, and giant size. The best families accept these dogs as more than

just pets. They see their Newfoundlands as members of the family. With good care, Newfs will live an average of eight to ten years.

Puppies are born blind and deaf. About 10 to 14 days after birth, their ear canals and eyes begin to open.

GLOSSARY

American Kennel Club - an organization that studies and promotes interest in purebred dogs.

breed - a group of animals sharing the same ancestors and appearance. A breeder is a person who raises animals. Raising animals is often called breeding them.

Canidae (KAN-uh-dee) - the scientific Latin name for the dog family. Members of this family are called canids. They include domestic dogs, wolves, jackals, foxes, and coyotes.

diverse - made up of unlike pieces or qualities.

flews - the hanging side parts of a dog's upper lips.

heatstroke - a condition marked by a lack of sweating, high body temperature, and fainting. It is caused by extended exposure to high temperatures.

litter - all of the puppies born at one time to a mother dog.

muzzle - an animal's nose and jaws.

neuter (NOO-tuhr) - to remove a male animal's reproductive organs.

pregnant - having one or more babies growing within the body.

socialize - to accustom an animal or a person to spending time with others.

spay - to remove a female animal's reproductive organs.

vaccine (vak-SEEN) - a shot given to animals or humans to prevent them from getting an illness or a disease.

WEB SITES

To learn more about Newfoundlands, visit ABDO Publishing Company on the World Wide Web at **www.abdopublishing.com**. Web sites about Newfoundlands are featured on our Book Links page. These links are routinely monitored and updated to provide the most current information available.

INDEX